SOULFUL GROUP –
Garden

Richard C. Bower is a celebrated writer, poet, and journalist. He has worked with the BBC, OCD UK, and Gitanjali and Beyond amongst many others. Accredited by UNESCO Nottingham City of Literature, and a member of the prestigious Authors' Club (as was Oscar Wilde et al), Richard C. Bower's An Expedition Around My Garden advocates the empowering energy that exists in the natural world - one that ultimately binds all living beings together. The book highlights how we are all connected and cultivates a consciousness that can be shared between us all in every moment of every single day. A refreshing torchbearer of hope and inspiration, An Expedition Around My Garden believes in the positive flow of goodness and natural energy that ultimately binds us all together as one. Originally from Mansfield, Richard and his work have recently been celebrated as part of the very first Nottinghamshire Day, and his work is being critiqued in classrooms around the world.

An Expedition Around My Garden – A Literal, Personal & Philosophical Journey.

The right of Richard C. Bower to be identified as the author of this work has been asserted by him in accordance with the Copyright, Designs and Patents Act 1988.

First Published in 2023 by Soulful Group
we unlace words & detangle life to help make the world a more soulful place.

www.soulfulgroup.com

Cover artwork by Natalie Mosley.

ISBN- 978-1-8381149-8-5

OTHER BOOKS BY RICHARD C. BOWER

POSTMODERN
Sanctuary
Pleasures In The Pathless Woods

'An Insight Into The Cover'

In the cover the 'central' focus point is the bench, which is eclipsed by a burst of sunlight to illustrate that this is where the 'magic' happens. The bench is black as it forms no colour against the bright sunlight; the psychedelic colours then merging into an array of bright fusion. Sat perched on the bench is a bird - illustrating the book's connection with nature. Stirring imagination and intrigue, the cover radiates with a kaleidoscopic energy - all emanating from what is to be found inside!

An Expedition Around My Garden – A Literal, Personal & Philosophical Journey.

Richard C. Bower

To my Mum & Dad

X

FOREWORD

The Immortal Touch of Thy Hands: Nature illumines the Poet

Fill my heart, quench my thirst,

Grant me the exuberance of life.

In your universe, your mansion,

Give me a spacious abode.

More light, more light,

Pour light into those eyes, O Lord,

Fill my flute with divine tunes,

Grant me a flood of melodies (Bose 2).

On 3 June 1912, while sailing through the Red Sea, Rabindranath Tagore had written this song (Pal 308); and the next morning as he stood on the deck he had a divine experience of the mild cold breeze which came as a blessing like a call from the different directions of the universe which appeared to embody the eternal. The poet could connect with the phenomenal world and experience *'yat kincha yadidam sarvam prana ejati nihsritam'*: 'all that there is comes out of life and vibrates in it' (*The Religion of Man* 54).

Tagore's religion was based on his realisation of the infinite, which began

> its journey from the impersonal *dyaus*, 'the sky', wherein light had its manifestation; then came to Life, which represented the force of self-creation in time, and ended in *purushah*, the 'Person', in whom dwells timeless love (Ibid.).

This principle involves a pure enjoyment of knowledge as it nurtures the seeds of freedom through which our life facilitates a process of acculturation which involves affiliating the 'distinct, even disjunct' with the other in the spirit of a 'right to difference in equality' (Bhabha 56, xx). It involves a change of our frame of mind which permits us to abandon thoughts and ideas supporting monocultural points of views for an intellectual and creative openness that enables an understanding of 'freedom through cultivating a mutual sympathy' ("Freedom" 628) towards creating 'habits of coexistence' (Appiah xix). This vindicates the need for an international approach of associating human beings with each other through non-violence by erasing the shadow lines of conflict, emphasizing our obligation to one another (Ibid. xvi) in this globalised world with a 'real heterogeneity of interests and identities' (Nayar 180).

Richard C. Bower's *An Expedition Around My Garden: A Literal, Personal and Philosophical Journey* is a singular experience for all sensitive minds who explore, beyond differences the truth that lies in nature 'apparell'd in celestial light,/the glory and the freshness of a dream' (Wordsworth 587) with spirit, life and colour. The symphony in the narrative is woven with the judicious use of fresh and lively images, and the vibrant colours affirm 'him, transcend the limits of mortality – not in duration of time, but in perfection of truth' (*The Religion of Man* 55). Through his intense explorations in his garden, Bower has attained the fullness of his personality, becoming one with nature and humanity. His experiences are universal, and a close reading of the novel enables us to concentrate and be conscious of our existence, as 'the joy of unity within ourselves, seeking expression, becomes creative; whereas our desire for the fulfilment of our needs is constructive' (*Creative Unity* 495).

The spirit of truth is further enlivened through the author's observation which is a result of his oneness with nature, making him a naturalist and a humanist. Through his impressions we discover his philosophy of life which ascertains the 'unity and significance on all the joy and sorrow and circumstance of life' by interrogating all shadow-lines of race, nation, class, gender, caste, or creed, threading into a harmonious whole the various forms of the self through which an individual can experience the unity within the universe. This is a reflection of Rabindranath Tagore's concept of the realisation of the 'Jiban Debata' (*Of Myself* 7), the Lord of his Being (Fraser 116). Following the Vedic 'Aabirabirnya edhi' (*Selected Essays* 262) and inspired by nature, Bower has been able to include humanity in one spiritual circle through the purview of his creativity. *An Expedition Around My Garden* is an endeavour to assimilate with nature and experience the bliss which enables him to explore the realms of freedom and share with his readers the philosophic realisation of the great human truth that

> our mind and our words come away baffled from the supreme Truth, but he who knows That, through the immediate joy of his own soul, is saved from all doubts and fears (*Angel of Surplus* 6, 7).

'We are in an exceptionally new situation, but elements of older experiences may clarify our vision if one finds the proper means of access', commented Alan Wald on Enzo Traverso's *Fire and Blood: The European Civil War, 1914-1945* (2017). If we compare this to the reality of 2020-2021, a reflective consideration of the pandemic and the way it has been managed by science and medicine, becomes a decisive factor in an inspection of the role literature plays in society as we endeavour to affirm the latter's persistent relevance. Being a part of the Gaia system,[1] the Covid-19 pandemic confined us in our homes as a result of our ecological arrogance, thus emphasizing the necessity for human beings to be conscious of their activities which should nourish society and the economy in order to meet the demands of the present without endangering the needs of the future. It has made us introspect on the rights of nature as well as on sustainable development in our life processes; Bower's personal explorations in *An Expedition Around My Garden* comes with a special aesthetic appeal that invites the reader to decipher the living image of beauty in nature and its vitality which thrives in and offers peace and tranquillity manifested in life. This timely publication emphasizes the need to bond with nature for an aesthetic experience which lends truth to our very existence. The philosophical experiences documented in the thirty-seven chapters recall William Wordsworth's 'Lines Composed a Few Miles above Tintern Abbey, On Revisiting the Banks of The Wye During a Tour. July 13, 1798' where, 'Nature never did betray / The heart that loved her' with 'acts of kindness and of love' as its 'influence' is 'powerful and transformative' (Wordsworth 206, 207). Through the author's experiences, the reader can not only relate to, but also realize that with a 'quest of external success our works become unspiritual and unexpressive' as we fail to discover the 'aspect of unity', on being 'driven to distraction by our pursuit of the fragmentary' (*Creative Unity* 496). Besides the author's philosophical awakening, the novel also facilitates the reader's journey towards the realisation that the 'truth of our life depends upon our attitude of mind towards it' – an attitude which, with the passage of time, positively assists the 'special circumstance of our surroundings and our temperaments'. It validates our endeavours to vindicate correlations with the universe 'either by conquest or by union, either through the cultivation of power or through that of sympathy' (Ibid. 511). The beauty of the garden - its amity and peace - ensure harmony amidst the contrary forces which might otherwise mar the rhythm of life, and as the author perceives this rhythm, he is enlightened by the 'divine being, the world-worker, who is the Great Soul ever dwelling inherent in the hearts of all people' (*The Religion of Man* 55). This realisation is like a kindle which the reader shares with the writer, a divine consciousness which through the

Open doors, break[ing] down barriers,

Rescue me, grant me deliverance.

More love, more love,

Let my ego be drowned.

In a torrent of nectar

Give more, more, more of your Self (Bose 2, 3).

An Expedition Around My Garden is Richard C. Bower's epiphanic realisation of the truth in nature which affirms 'Peace is true...Love is true...; and Truth is the One' (*Creative Unity* 500). It reminds us of a similar experience by Rabindranath Tagore, after which, he wrote that

> some ancient mist had in a moment lifted from my sight, and the morning light on the face of the world revealed an inner radiance of joy. The invisible screen of the commonplace was removed from all things and all men, and their ultimate significance was intensified in my mind; and this is the definition of beauty (*The Religion of Man* 80).

The result was 'Nirjharer Swapnabhanga' (The Awakening of the Waterfall), a testament to his ability to spiritually connect with everything in Nature. Like Wordsworth, it was the moment when Tagore seemed to see into the life of things (Fraser 75). Richard C. Bower's understanding of the immediacy and intensity of nature's wealth is similar to Wordsworth and Tagore's experience, and his ability to mix the variety of colours of nature to embody his distinctive expressionistic style and convincingly share his understanding of the philosophy of life, signify his acute sensibilities and cosmopolitanism, his *mukti*, the freedom of truth.

Ulrich Beck refers to 'risk society', where 'we live in the age of unintended consequences' (*Risk Society* 22), where massive modernization's ecological arrogance has accelerated climate change and global warming, suffocating the earth with the insensible, and selfish acts of human beings. *An Expedition Around My Garden: A Literal, Personal and Philosophical Journey* is the endeavour of a conscious artist to address this crisis in civilization through the philosophical revelation engendered by nature, which every sensitive reader will surely enjoy and remember as the 'source' of unmitigated light even 'as twilight fades into evening and evening dissolves in night', ushering a profound pristine solace 'smoothly through silence' (Gupta 99). Like the divine presence in nature, this book will shine in this world as it,

Set[s] my life to music

Play your melody of the light at dawn in my life.

The tune that fills your wordless songs, and a child's flute of life.

Smiling at its mother's face – make me the instrument of that tune.

Adorn me,

Adorn me in the dress that adorns the dust of this earth.

The rhythmic beauty of the evening malati, adorned in its secret aroma,

The decoration that joyfully forgets itself, embellish me in that adornment (Bose 12).

1. Endnote:

James Lovelock's Gaia theory suggests that the Earth's organisms and their inorganic surroundings are intimately blended to form a single and self-regulating complex system, nurturing the conditions for life on the planet. Gaia is unstoppable and wild when it suits her for the sake of the Earth's wellbeing. Lovelock is of the opinion that Covid-19 is a part of the Gaia system of self-regulation to level an overcrowded world and ensure that food supplies are adequate for all.

Works Cited:

Anthony Appiah, Kwame. *Cosmopolitanism: Ethics In A World of Strangers*. England: Penguin Books, 2006. Print.

Beck, Ulrich. *Risk Society: Towards a New Modernity*. Trans. Mark Ritter. London: Sage Publications, 2019. Print.

Bhabha, Homi. *The Location of Culture*. London and New York: Routledge Classics, 2019. Print.

Bose, Sugata. Trans. *Tagore The World Voyager*. India: Random House, 2013, 2. Print.

Fraser, Bashabi. *Rabindranath Tagore*. London: Reaktion Books, 2019. Print.

Gupta, Tapati. *Transient*. Bolpur: Birutjatio Sahitya Sammiloni, 2021. Print.

Nayar, Pramod K. *Contemporary Literary and Cultural Theory*. NewDelhi: Pearson, 2013. Print.

Pal, Prasantakumar. *Rabijibani* Vol. V. Kolkata: Ananda Publishers, 2018. Print.

Tagore, Rabindranath. *Gitanjali: Song Offerings.* London: The Chiswick Press for The India Society, 1912. Print.

Tagore, Rabindranath. *Angel of Surplus: Some Essays and Addresses on Aesthetics.* Calcutta: Visva-Bharati, 1978. Print.

Tagore, Rabindranath. *The Religion of Man* (1930). New Delhi: Rupa Publications India Pvt. Ltd., 2005. Print.

Tagore, Rabindranath Tagore. "Freedom." *The English Writings of Rabindranath Tagore* Vol. 4. Ed. Nityapriya Ghosh. New Delhi: Sahitya Akademi, 2007. 627 - 628. Print.

Tagore, Rabindranath. *Of Myself.* Trans. D. Joardar and J. Winter. Kolkata: Visva Bharati Publishing Department, 2009. Print.

Tagore, Rabindranath. *Creative Unity. The English Writings of Rabindranath Tagore* Vol. 2. Ed. Sisir Kumar Das. New Delhi: Sahitya Akademi, 2014. 493 - 569. Print.

Tagore, Rabindranath. *Selected Essays on Aesthetics*. Ed. and Trans. Amitabha Chaudhury. New Delhi: Sahitya Akademi, 2016. Print.

Wald, Alan. "Fascinating Antifascism: Alan Wald on Enzo Traverso's *Fire and Blood*." Verso, 05 July 2016. Web. 25 December 2021.

Wordsworth, William. *The Collected Poems of William Wordsworth*. Great Britain: The Wordsworth Poetry Library, 1994. Print.

Dr Saptarshi Mallick
Assistant Professor for English
Sukanta Mahavidyalaya
University of North Bengal
Associate Editor, *Gitanjali and Beyond*
Scottish Centre of Tagore Studies (ScoTs)

INTRODUCTION

Through my role at Nottingham UNESCO City of Literature, there is what we refer to as an 'Unholy Trinity' of writers we frequently look back to. These are George Gordon Byron, David Herbert Lawrence, and Alan Sillitoe. Each a writer of striking originality and style, but who are inextricably linked in history. Not just through geography - though all three lived within a ten-mile radius of the other, albeit over two centuries - but through what they represent. Each was a rebel.

Kicking against the pricks is something Notts excels in. We are a fiery place, being where the English Civil War began when Charles I took a gamble and raised his standard at Nottingham Castle, demanding fealty to the Crown. The gamble backfired, and soon Charles was to lose that Crown - as well as the head it perched upon.

The Luddites - now, unfairly, a byword for those who can't get Netflix streaming, but actually a group of men desperately fighting against the destruction of their livelihoods by mindless capitalism - started their campaign of frame breaking here (Byron would devote his maiden speech to the Lords to defend these men).

We've had riots: cheese riots, bread riots, theatre riots. When our parliamentary 'representative' failed to support the Reform Bill in 1831, we set his house alight. As his house was Nottingham Castle, this was a big deal.

Even our most famous legendary figure, that proto-socialist in Lincoln Green, is now a global icon of egalitarianism and fighting for what is right.

Our writers reflect this facet of the Notts psyche. The Unholy Trinity all, in their own way, blazed a trail with righteous fire; stood up to tyranny and refused to be categorised and filed away and forgotten about. To quote Sillitoe's raging Saturday Night, Sunday Morning anti-hero Arthur Seaton "Whatever you say I am, that's what I'm not".

And so to today. Notts is a more peaceful place, and one of relative prosperity. The mines and heavy industry have gone, and the Universities have become the major drivers of economic and cultural change. Our reputation has shifted - we're now seen as somewhere almost magically creative and cool, icons such as Sir Paul Smith and Vicky McClure lending the place a sense of identity that feels as comfortable on the pages of an international fashion magazine as it does the inky sheets of the Nottingham Post.

So has that fire been dampened down over time? Has that distinct streak of self-determinism run its course? Have we stopped raging against the world and all that try to impose their will on it? As the lace looms clattered to a halt, as the last chunk of anthracite coal was gouged deep below the hills, did we switch off?

Not at all. That fire still burns hot, that streak still courses. Writers such as Richard C. Bower demonstrate that our creativity is innate. His writing within pulls from a rich body of influences spanning centuries and continents, yet is firmly rooted in the here, the now. His visions are expansive, yet focused. There is an understanding that writing - or more accurately, *words* - are liberating, they are challenging, they have the power to change ourselves and change the world. If in the right hands, they can work wonders, something we have seen multiple times over the history of Notts. Reading contemporary writers such as Richard C. Bower, I'm confident that long after all who currently walk this earth are but dust, that fire will rage on, that spirit will remain undimmed.

Matt Turpin
UNESCO
Nottingham City of Literature

AUTHOR'S INTRODUCTION

An Expedition Around My Garden is the experience and expression of pure energy - an energy that loves life in every form that it appears, an energy that does not judge what it encounters, an energy that perceives meaningfulness and purpose in the smallest details of the nature that surrounds us. Every single moment is potent with possibility and when we align our thoughts, emotions, and actions with the highest part of ourselves we are filled with enthusiasm, purpose, and meaning. Life is rich and full. We have no thoughts of bitterness. We are joyously and intimately engaged with our world.

AUTHOR'S NOTE

What follows is based on actual occurrences and must be regarded in its essence as fact.

"The real voyage of discovery consists not in seeing new landscapes but in having new eyes."

- Proust

"If the doors of perception were cleansed everything would appear to man as it is, infinite."

- *William Blake*

I

It is often fascinating when beginning a new venture, and to offer the world an insight, in the same way that life beholds to us all a rich tapestry of delights.

I offer you, the reader, such pleasure right here in this book. I have embarked upon, and brought to fruition, a voyage of discovery around my garden. The absorbing considerations I have made, and the continuous delight I encountered on the way, pervaded me with the inclination to write about it; the conviction of it being put to good use was a considerable influence. I feel contentment when I consider the numerous despondent individuals to whom I am here presenting an asset against ennui, and an assuage of the misfortunes they feel bound by. The joy you discover in an expedition around my garden is sheltered from the ill at ease nature of others; it is self-sufficient from the volatility of chance and fortune.

After all, is there any individual so despondent, so forsaken, that they do not have a small lair into which they can remove themselves and shelter away from everybody?

I am certain that any reasonable person will embrace this book and be inclined to approve of the expedition I put forth.

II

As I start writing, a blackbird sings its punctuation – as though praising the expedition I am about to begin. As the title suggests, all you need to undertake the expedition is a garden – or your local park. Thus, it can immediately be admired and celebrated by most. And, what a rehabilitating journey for those who may be ill! To breathe in the mild air and vibrancy of the garden! This is for everybody inspired to do so from following my precedent. Would those with even the most languid demeanour be reluctant to set forth with me to derive a rapture so easily obtainable? So, liven up and let us proceed! Join me – everybody and anybody who has been subjected to a multitude of life's chagrin. May all the despondent, ill, and exhausted individuals of the world join me for the journey. May all the indolent come to light as a whole! Let us surrender happily to the beauty of nature in the garden, and let our inspiration fly on the wings to wherever the birds may take us.

III

My garden is located on the 53rd degree latitude and 1st degree longitude, at an elevation above sea level of 106 metres. Without treading on its decorative borders, the perimeter of the gardens irregular shape measures at 93 steps. Yet the expedition will cover immeasurably more than this, as I traverse it habitually from hawthorn to blackberry bush, or even through my mind while sitting, as I am, on the garden bench and taking in the surroundings. The blue cloudless sky is the limit with my imagination unfurled to each notion, encounter and feeling. I am enthused to experience all that appears… as though I am walking, receiving pleasures, through a pathless wood! There is so much joy, all abundant, that you need to take your time and appreciate all that is around. I believe there is an appealing quality when pursuing a pure notion anywhere it may go – just like the huntsman follows his game, in the absence of attempting to remain on any pre-determined route. And so, when I journey around the garden, I seldom adhere to a direct path: I go from the flowerbed towards the bird table; from there I set forth indirectly to the raised wooden decking area, where I stand for a while, before making my way back and sitting down once more on the garden bench. It is an old unpainted bench – perfect to sit back, watch, and listen… as I feel the rays of an early spring sun charge the atmosphere with a sense of purity and calm. Throughout the recent chill of winter, I would witness the snow-white paradise, and enjoy the intense silence that fell around me. Then following the peace, the serenity, and the quietude an inner warmth arose – a feeling of spring being conjured within. What a delight – it inspires me to write… and as time slowly melts, its passage has taken me someplace else.

IV

When leaving the garden bench, in a short due
east direction, I arrive onto the lawn, which is at
the centre of the garden: it is like an enchanting
carpet beneath my feet, a most pleasing vision.
As the day awakens, I can see the dawn – it is
contagious; rapidly spreading as the sun rises,
cavorting itself with the plants and with the
trees. I see vivid colours, in leaves and in
flowers, amid patterns rejoicing in the garden. I
listen to the birds, listening to every musical
verse, as they jump merrily on their perch in
their chosen habitat of the tall hawthorn bushes.
Just then a number of joyful thoughts sweep
through my mind; and I feel alive in a delightful
and tranquil way.

Here in these saccharine times, as such, I enjoy
relaxing a while by focussing my attention on the
here and now, becoming intensely conscious of
the present moment. The garden is an
auditorium, inducing the mind to awaken with
delicate and pleasurable thoughts, that spread
into the narrative like euphoria – passing into a
world of the imagination, like when meeting a
virtue – a wonderful person, for the very first
time! And the flower bed is stirred with elation,

the air tinged with the edge of spring as it scrawls its magical calligraphy into the petals of daffodils. It is here that solitary pleasures give birth to flights of fancy and stir aspiration within me. Just then a blackbird lands right next to me, all content and calm as we make eye contact – a fascinating situation – before it joyfully fly's off into its freedom!

V

I similarly feel liberated. It is easy to be swept up in the constant noise of the conditioned mind, that is full of negative and self-perpetuating thoughts. Out here in the garden, I am able to switch these thoughts off – I recognize they are there, and by doing so I see that they are separate from me. This realisation is like entering another dimension, as one is then able to sense a conscious presence of one's self, that lays beneath the distracting content of thought.

The self and one's thoughts are so closely intertwined, and so deeply ingrained, that it is easy to think they are one and the same entity. But through intelligent observation, and the meditative exercise stated above – in which the garden offers a highly conducive place to practice this art – stresses of the mind can be alleviated by simply breathing and distancing one's self from such thoughts. As this realisation occurs, watch as they subside into the distance and soon lose control over you!

VI

The mind is a tool, an instrument. It is there to be used and achieve specific objectives, and then afterwards it can be lay to rest for a while. I often use the artistry of the mind to transport me to other places. And with a pen to hand, I like to see where the journey takes me.

Writing is just one form of personal expression. I particularly find it therapeutic. Especially while I am sat and inspired by the sun as it shines its light on to a cast of vibrant shades and hues in the garden. And with a continuing fascination, I am suddenly exploring affinities with the sublime. Joyful is the writer for whom the ardour of nature steers one's solitary pleasures, who is able to express on sheets of white paper the sensation and a shift in emotion stirred within. Navigating from melancholy to wonder, through a landscape of loss to inspiring moments - drawn to mountains, glaciers, forests, the ocean! All such visions arise in the mind and are mirrored in ones writing. And with a gentle ease, the air - all keen, is clear and abundant, all intoxicating - caressing the body, shaking up the greenery! The mind liberates itself along such roads, that run cunningly away from last night's mist and yesterday's scars; towards supernal greens of a country view that are replicated in the trees as I open my eyes and my fastidious sight then takes in great pleasure!

VII

I wish for such notions described before to present you, the reader, with a lot to consider, and offer you a perception into which you can formulate your own dazzling encounters: you will not be disappointed if, on occasion, you succeed in liberating your mind to explore by itself; the relaxations that this ability will allow you will triumph over any other inferior concept. It can be profoundly rewarding to expand one's mind, and very being, in this manner, to inhabit great joy while remaining in the present moment, and thus to be content with one's lot.

If you endeavour to take flight from, and master, any notions of limitation your fulfilment will be boundless.

VIII

Throughout, the expedition remains as my
physical body is sat upright on the garden bench,
the soles of both feet firmly grounded on the
paving stone beneath. I remain motionless,
tuning in my awareness to all five senses. I notice
a solitary bird, a sparrow, cheekily thriving
between the branches of a hawthorn bush. Its
chirruping a stark beauty that compliments the
otherwise peaceful habitat. The wind blusters
around my ears, rustling up the hedges as the
tips of my eyelashes are tinted with the golden
glow of sunshine, heralding its swift arrival, as it
briefly blinds my sight, reflecting onto my face
and into my eyes. The day is abruptly brightened
with colour as the sun wavers, jauntily conferring
its presence as it stretches itself across the
horizon, while occupying the heights of my mind
and conveying a soothing sensation around my
body.

I feel enraptured, though there is a chill in the air
that encases a slight melancholy and gathers like
the sediment of a former memory. But, just then,
the sparrow reappears - accompanied by another
- and suddenly the focus returns with the
sunshine residing in my mind! This unexpected

moment caused space and time to fade, as I was transported to my younger days, and I could see my mother smiling as I kicked a football enthusiastically around the garden! What a memory, what a reflection – although fleeting, it was striking – and then in a flicker of an eye, the dream-like vision was gone.

IX

Let me now take the opportunity to describe to you the vision of the flower beds. It is true how the impact of colours affects us – they can enhance one's mood or depress us with their very tones. As it is only the beginning of spring, the colours in the decorative beddings are slightly muted, but still there is the cherry tree, with its fruit – coloured red, that represents power and courage. I see a lot of green, a renewal of life as it breathes, all ubiquitous surrounding the garden around its edge, and here and there one can see the faint dashes of yellow - a colour dedicated to joy, happiness, and optimism – as the heads of the daffodils begin to sprout through. Then there's the variegated plants exhibiting different colours; of white – an inherently positive colour, representing purity and innocence; green – with its healing powers; and purple – which symbolizes magic, mystery, stability, and energy!

And then I close my eyes. I see imprints on the back of my eyelids. I see stars - red, blue, and green - iridescent colours passing across. Like living jewellery, luminous inwardly, breathing and flowing with the same life that is in me.

As all is aligned, evoking a sense of beauty, like the teeth of a beautiful woman as she smiles - transposing exuberance, as everything comes alive within this moment!

And what a wonderful moment it is! One in which to let its vibrant energy radiate into the world … and leave this chapter where it is!

X

… … … The smile nestles, dazzling golden, on the meandering trees leaves. A delicious reflection, hearing nature as she breathes… … …!

XI

I am especially dedicated to meditating and reflecting while in the welcoming comfort of the garden. Surrounded by the positive colours, it generates an immense joy of which I am grateful to receive.

I also gain great pleasure from the song of the birds that accompanies me while doing so. The dawn chorus is like a feathered alarm clock, and I often rise early to listen. The day is fine, with clear weather and little wind, though a little cold so I am dressed appropriately in warm clothes. The birds are singing well, their chorus peaking around half-an-hour after sunrise. There is a variety of song from each different species, and I find it enjoyable to watch the variety of the performers as each take their turn on stage!

The first birds begin to sing about an hour before sunrise. By listening carefully, I notice that there is a regular sequence, with some species habitually starting before others. Among the earliest to rise are skylarks, song thrushes, robins, and blackbirds. Wrens and warblers seem to take a more relaxed approach and appear in the garden later. These smaller birds, who are perhaps more sensitive to the coldness of dawn, feed on insects that themselves appear later in the morning.

The dim light of dawn is not a good time to go foraging and singing also brings the risk of attracting a predator, so it is perhaps better done before the bright morning light betrays the birds' location. The air is often still at this time and, with less background noise, their song can carry much further afield, which helps them to attract a mate. But as daylight strengthens food becomes easier to find, and the hungry birds begin to move off, the resulting chorus thus gradually diminishing.

XII

The voices of spring keep on coming. The time is 18:07 and I have returned outside to sit on my bench. The evening air is calm and still, it is peaceful. Perfect to realign one's mind after a busy day. I have returned with the purpose of hearing another chorus – this time, the chorus of dusk. It is considerably quieter than the one at dawn this morning. Some birds, I have noticed, seem to prefer to sing at this time of day – like blue tits as they hop around, and tree sparrows - of which there's an ensemble of half a dozen congregated in one of the hawthorn bushes, all singing merrily together! At first their song sounds like white noise, all twittering and chirping together, and it is hard to separate one from the other. But the more you listen, the more you hear them as individuals and, once again, the garden suddenly becomes even richer as it is surrounded by all these characters! And then a blackbird joins in, with its song that is sung with a quality of honey in its voice. The blackbird's song, even though it is the end of day, has filled my ears with sunshine!

XIII

It is my intention to describe to you, the reader, my garden expedition as lucidly as I can – at least enough to enable you an enlightening comprehension of the experience. Whether setting off to ascend the highest peak of a mountain or, conversely, when exploring the zenith of a stream's trough, I feel it is important as a writer to convey the imagery as accurately as one can: the number of birds, the number of tree's, the colours of the flowers, the degrees of the garden corresponding to the north and south geographic poles of the earth, as well as the meridians, which are the half-circles running from pole to pole – all such things, including the time that dawn breaks which, today, was 06:24. I have always made notes of certain experiences and journeys throughout my life – writing in note pads, journals or diaries whenever on holiday or on weekends away. And it is with the proposition of informing the reader of the experiences gained from such journeys, that I have chosen to write about, and share, this very expedition.

XIV

Standing, bare-footed, in the centre of the lawn, I vocalise a "good morning" to the world and focus the direction of the sentiment to the life and energy resplendent in the garden. The feeling I reciprocate is empowering, as I outstretch my arms in a welcoming manner and feel the warmth of the sunshine as it smiles upon my face. And in this moment, that is beautiful - that stimulates light and makes things visible – I contemplate life, and how it is a journey in itself. And inside, I rise, as I feel the affection of the sun - this view of life could have passed me by had I not opened my eyes and witnessed, but even so, things are real and magical even if I could not see them! And the sincerity of gratitude washes over me, like a reaction all around my mind and body, as I feel the biochemical charge of energy released within! And stood here, on the lawn, bare-footed - I realise, in this very moment, how everything is synchronised!

XV

The garden, as I have touched upon, is decorated with trees, plants, and flowers that make it more than aesthetically pleasing on the eye. Upon leaving my bench and walking in a south-east direction, I will lead you to the beginning of the bedding display and point out each plant while heading around the garden's perimeter in a clockwise direction. At the beginning of the border, quite aptly, are a host of golden daffodils, serving as a reminder to the arrival of spring as they flutter and dance in the breeze. They have a beautiful shape and fragrance and symbolize the happiness of life, and it is a joy to welcome and appreciate them in the garden!

Moving along, to the elephant ear plant, a perennial plant which is appealing due to its large leathery, rounded leaves and dense, erect clusters of bell-shaped white flowers that bloom in spring.

Next is a blackberry bush which, as the season progresses, will begin to bear edible fruit. Also, according to tradition, it is said that the blackberry's deep purple colour represents the blood of Christ with his crown resplendent of the thorns from the branches of the bush.

To the side of the blackberry bush is a small cherry tree, which has a dense shrubby growth habit, and is smothered with large single white flowers. The anthers of the flowers are a visibly vibrant red which stand out in contrast to the white petals. In winter, the tree possesses a certain beauty with its distinctive silhouette that stands against the dark sky.

The cherry tree is joined by the reliable qualities of the plum tree, which reward one with the deliciously plump harvest of its fruit, which is ripe for eating straight from the tree!

Beneath these trees are another splash of golden coloured daffodils, as though scattered from the hand of Jackson Pollock. They stand at the foot of a couple of humble apple trees as one continues around the gardens border. Similar to the plum trees, there is nothing sweeter than popping into the garden and picking your own apples!

Next is a further blackberry bush, followed by the trimmed appearance of a lilac tree, with its pale purple, pink and white flowering that blooms in late spring. Complimenting this colouring is the 'Queen of Climbers', clematis that climbs over the fence behind and produces a mass of flowers in a wide variety of shapes and colours! There is so much here to get lost in and explore, and I am only halfway around the garden, but the rest I will leave for later and let you enjoy, along with me, the imagery thus far presented!

XVI

The garden is like a snapshot of well-being in the charming encompassment of spring! To witness natures roots flourishing generates a peaceful aura within. Mother nature is like a beautiful woman, shining brightly in her gown while adorned in all her splendour throughout the garden spring. The evergreen conifer dances and weaves its limbs with the hawthorn bushes and crab apple tree, both - either side - adjoining; with songbirds trilling among the greenery; insects fluttering amid the blossoming floret; every single thing purring with energy and delight! And at night, the enlightening snow moon holds sway, as it waves goodbye to winter and ushers in a new day.

As I sit, I envisage tomorrow's sunrise shining brightly in the skies of morn and anticipate mother nature as she heralds in a new phase, with her sunlight thriving boundless throughout the skyline!

XVII

These pages, these words, are full of energy as ink swims between inspiration and expression – asserting a sense of belonging as the narrative ripples with nature, running like a thread through life like a vein on the map of my insides, before breathing, as they do, on reams of white paper. I trust that they convey a most joyful outlook, and I hope you discover them to your approval!

XVIII

I sit contentedly beneath the trees at the far end
of the garden, who welcome me like a loyal
companion. I sit and enjoy the silence for a short
period of time. I observe a dragonfly hovering –
its wings horizontal – as it feeds on a haze of
mosquitos. Winter seems like a distant memory
– its persona having been overthrown by the sun
that has suddenly turned things golden! I enjoy
the warmth of harmony as it builds from within
and without me, the weekend's crescendo
peaking on this Sunday evening that began with
the sweet-smelling perfume of yesterday's
sunrise, that I now sit and reflect upon in my
own personal haven while resting my mind and
body.

XIX

I am aware that my writing conveys an incredibly positive aura. This is to my satisfaction as I have been taking in such pleasurable things, and as I do I begin to take note of them - I enjoy the experience and make mental notes, before then writing them down on paper shortly afterwards. Today, the climate I board upon is more composed, which is conducive to subduing one's thoughts and to realign them after the heights they have experienced from the ingratiating first days of spring - although it is not always easy to descend from the altitudes one has just climbed!

I would like to think that the absorbing considerations I have made, and the continuous delights I encounter on the way will enable you, the reader, to love your surroundings and nature more – that my writing captures her essence and reveals her secrets; and I hope that it enables you to see, and experience, things that may have previously escaped your observation!

So, one hopes, my contemplations will thrill for generations to come just as the music that inhabits the skies has illuminated the world since the beginning of time.

XX

The music in the garden is sacred and moves me with its abundantly fresh and never-failing melodies. It makes one feel delight upon hearing it, with its captivating harmonies that cannot fail to touch all incarnate beings, providing a vehicle for voyages to other worlds - be it a spiritual, mystical, or magical dimension.

Upon hearing and feeling such resonance, one's consciousness is able to voyage at great will, like an awakening that leads us beyond mere entertainment or emotional stimulus.

XXI

The day is calm and filled with a quiet gladness,
although mid-afternoon is heralded with a
sudden commotion as a number of blackbirds
descend upon the hawthorn bushes before
vanishing impossibly, just as quickly.

I sit in the shadow of the day and contemplate
the similar disposition of the recently planted
parsley, with its seeds residing in the partial
shade of an ornamental garden container. I
consider the parallels of physical and spiritual
growth, and how both are nurtured best when in
the right environment.

Each day, upon entering the garden, I
acknowledge the parsley moss curled 2 herb and
look forward to the day its leaves are deeply
cultivated, with its vigorous and compact curls
on show. That day will come with the
blossoming of time, but one must follow first
the patient and faithful duties of feeding and
watering the plant to enable its growth. Growth
generates high regard, but it isn't all about what's
happening above the surface. At this juncture I
again recognise the commonalities I share with
the plants in the garden, and how all need to

establish strong roots before they are then able to flourish.

XXII

When one plants parsley, or anything, in the garden, if it does not grow well the parsley is not to blame. One should look for reasons as to why it is not doing well. It may need less sun, it may need more water, or it may need some compost. The parsley is not to blame. Yet, if we have a problem and fall-out with somebody – be it a family member, a friend, or an acquaintance – we tend to blame the other person. But if we know how to take care of them, they will grow – like the parsley. And one, I feel, can also take solace, personally, in this – when the aim is to work towards something as opposed to working against it. Applying blame has no positive effect at all on the parsley – in fact, it is dysfunctional. This affinity with the parsley is my reflection of the day. No blame, no argument, just understanding. Through understanding, a situation can change – for the better – and bring with it growth. Not just for the parsley, but for all!

XXIII

During the expedition I am naturally exposed to the sense impressions characterized by the garden, and I have thus allowed a small number of people an insight into the resplendent joys of the journey. I have conveyed the awe-inspiring expedition to some select confidantes and arbiters of taste – to an artist, a musician, to a university lecturer, and to my father - and one and all have expressed a feeling of calm and enjoyment in response to it: so true a reflection of the garden – just as nature intended!

What more could one ask for upon seeking a blessing, than the aforementioned confidantes serving as a reflection to the fruits of the expedition I presented them? And for everyone who experiences it, the magic of the garden is there for all, with its rich tapestry host to a vast number of valuable considerations to discover and reflect upon.

It is here that one can focus and gain understanding, it is here that one can realign and relax, it is here that one can inspire and be inspired, all while raising one's aspirations and contemplating life, the universe, and everything!

Throughout this voyage of discovery, one is able to observe many truths – as I sit and view the daffodils opposite and sense their buds sprouting inside. And I realise, the expedition around my garden is like holding an illuminating mirror up to one's self, and indeed it applies to us all. This vision, this realisation, serves in its richness of both depth and complexion.

And with this knowledge I give an appreciative look towards the garden, as I sit back, smile, and breathe in its inherent delights.

XXIV

In advance of progressing farther, I would like to address the circumstances in which it may appear this expedition has occurred.

I have not solely undertaken this voyage due to the world being subjected to a pandemic, which has then resulted in a national lockdown. I have plenty of other things I could be doing, and many things I could be writing about and working on. I believe life is a journey, and this expedition is always ready to manifest throughout our lives at any given moment, and I am of the opinion that my particular journey had begun way before the pandemic took hold.
I do believe, however, that this book would be ideal to read during these times due to the imposed withdrawal of the masses. But there is much more to this book, it is to be read at any point in life – and many times over. Like the garden, it contains rich depths with which many hidden treasures are just waiting to be discovered, and I highly recommend people should find time to read it, whatever their circumstances!

I am extremely grateful for the enriched emphasis these times have given to my expedition. The quietude of my garden is preferable to the commotion and anxiety of the outside world, that is widely inhabited with a lack of moderation and restraint.

XXV

The garden is modestly adorned. Two benches, three ornamental pots on a large wooden decking area (that needs painting), a bird bath and table, and a bird house on the upper regions of the wall of my abode. All of which depict a rather unostentatious elegance. This consideration endowed my satisfaction to become heightened, as my outlook is focussed on appreciation. And suddenly I am transported by the loud burst of a wren's song, interspersed with the short and fast descending rhythm of the chaffinch – and it is like I am surrounded with the tuneful duelling of a cello and flute, all while I remain seated on my bench! The sensation aroused within is one of elation, as though witnessing the vision of a delightful female dressed in the most fetching attire!

XXVI

Are people genuinely happy in this world we live? I favourably consider a shaft of light that shines on an open glade, in a land where trees and species flourish - as opposed to a mass consumer society, with its dreams that end in ruined plight. As I think on, I realise how subordinated we have all become and how the soul is overrun. The world is suffocating in work, commerce and conformity with grounds for misery far and wide. I contemplate solitude, and how it is conducive to creating a calm and meditative state, and - what if being alone was framed as an opportunity for developing one's self? As I stand, in the garden, I observe the geniality of a hyacinth as it enters the day – I note its colour and lively tone while an inner silence remains. And just then the landscape moves me. The sun, from behind the clouds, configures resilience as I stand alone. It is just me and the trees stood solemn in the breeze, as the clouds move onwards, I extend my gratitude upwards as rays of light shine through the clouds – onto new frontiers, and the imagined landscape of the open glade is suddenly transformed! And I relax, sit back, and feel a sense of happiness while breathing in the scent of narcissus flowers returning.

XXVII

As the sun shines, I hear the chorus of buds
sprouting – the rebirth of spring - in tune with
an expanse of clear blue sky on the horizon,
reflecting a serene sense of calm.

XXVIII

Spring is a fine time to be in the garden on a late afternoon. And it was about to get even better. Bounding over the neighbouring roof tops, I heard what sounded like a dog yapping in the sky. After tuning in my hearing, I realised it was some geese flying over the houses!

There is always debate about when spring begins. Meteorologically, it is pegged to March 1; this year, astronomical spring starts on March 20. In reality, each corner of the country has its own marker, from the celandines opening on your lanes, to the blue tits building garden nests or frogspawn hatching. Others consider it to be when the pink-footed geese start flying their gentle, shifting spear northwards – with their built-in mechanism of iron in their beaks that helps them navigate, like their very own built-in compass!

And with that, my mind is sent on a wild goose chase, exploring foreign climates!

XXIX

It is morning and today I feel like singing with the birds! I am particularly allured by the familiar sound of a wood pigeon that precedes the loud clatter of wings as it then flies away in a northerly direction. My gaze follows as it does, before returning and focussing on the remainder of the garden that I have yet to describe.

So, following on from the clematis where I left it in an earlier chapter, and continuing to walk in a clockwise direction, around the central lawn, past my bench and the stone walling, you then arrive at the second flower bed that adorns the garden. Along the ground, is a covering of hostas – plantain lilies – with their shade tolerant green foliage and loose clusters of tubular white flowers that stand on tall stems. The esteemed foliage is particularly attractive in the summer with its often scented and pretty bloom.

Standing above, and behind, the hostas are two blackberry bushes that mirror those standing at the opposite end of the garden. Next to these are the two taller hawthorn bushes. Its leaves, discrete ornamental flowering and cute berries are its main attractions, and it forms a defensive perimeter in its location of the garden. Nonetheless it is much more than that, since it has ornate leaves and blooms abundantly, making it a very beautiful tree. Its leaves take on varied hues from spring to fall, and it is decorated with magnificent marble-like berries from the end of summer until the beginning of winter. Even though they are edible, the berries of the hawthorn taste bland and mealy when raw, but birds go wild about them – which explains the trees popularity, as each day it is highly populated by them!

The berries have relaxing properties that are commonly used in natural healing preparations and it is said that this hardy medicinal plant, with very hard wood, was used by witches to ward off evil spirits! The hawthorn bush is celebrated for its health benefits and therapeutic value and, along with the berries, the shrub's leaves can be eaten too.

Next to these bushes is the distinctive conifer tree, that gives the garden a splash of lush dark-green dense foliage and goes bright light green in early summer.

Finally, standing next to the conifer, is a crab apple tree. Although modest in height, its abundant blossom and ornamental appeal of pretty fruitlets makes it a highly attractive feature of the garden!

What a delight it is to be in these beautiful surroundings, that convey such a joyful and tranquil place! One cannot help but feel full of warmth and be content with joy!

XXX

A slug slowly encroaches upon one of the small ornamental plantations, when abruptly the imagery of the parsleys vigorous and compact curls is on show! For it appears that what was once hidden in darkness, has suddenly found the light to grow!

XXXI

There are a few things I have yet to mention that are in the garden. On the surface they are nothing major, but their inclusion will tidy things up, at least in my mind! In the small far corner next to the aforementioned crab apple tree, there is a wheelbarrow and a small shed. The shed is naturally used for storage, as is the garage that stands alongside it. Both have in the expected items – a lawn mower, hedge trimmers, garden tools, etc. But I also view both the shed and the garage as large memory boxes. This is due to my own personal items stored in them from years gone by. So, for this expedition to be complete and include all of its riches, I will delve right here into my stored memories.

The shed contains music – boxes full of old cassettes from my younger days. Not only do they convey my varying tastes of genres, singers, artists, bands and albums throughout the years, but – as music magically does – each and every cassette possesses a magnitude of personal memories. They include former lovers, friends, hedonistic nights out, dancing, the fashion of attire I would be wearing at the time, haircuts, … shops, buildings, jobs, my youth, schools, university, towns, cities, holidays, acquaintances, … family, pets, neighbours, happiness, sorrow, sunshine, on and on and on - the list is endless!

The garage, similarly, is a treasure chest of memories, but in here they are stored in hundreds of books and vinyl records. As I delve into my collections, I am assaulted by a myriad of sounds, looks and smells from my past. Each and every one then grabs me by the hand as they weave their way through the labyrinth of my mind, and we dance our way through the passages and rhythms of former times!

XXXII

From the underlying theme of innocence, and all
invading presence of purity and growth, to one
of experience, knowledge and wisdom – this is
the immense landscape which I travel through in
all its bearings. I believe such an expedition
warrants one's time, and it is here that I elevate
my being.

The garden has served as a loyal companion and,
like a ship, transported me to eloquent lands of
inspiration and insight, while comforting me
with a sense of well-being.

I have discovered shores and heaths worthy of
salutation, while remaining in the refuge and
fortress of the garden.

So, when I desire a devoted view to rejoice with
all the vigour of my mind, I gallantly embrace
the fruits of my garden and yield to its delights.

XXXIII

I do not claim to be a botanist, but how I imagine the further delights of my expedition if I were – or to have one as my cohort! Either way, the presence in the garden beholds an effusively enthusiastic expression of feeling, with which my senses naturally tune in and re-establish an aura of balance. The sounds in the garden vibrate and intermingle in varying tones, providing a therapeutic ensemble of feelings and observations that shape my experience.

I sit on my bench – I feel at home here. The air is pristine, and time does not seem to exist beyond its mere concept. I live in the moment, through my senses and through the daylight. Just lately, the mornings greet me with a progressively glorious sunrise and the dawn chorus, once again, has me mesmerized – and I feel emotional as an adorably attentive blackbird approaches me within touching distance, as if it is saying "hello!" Yes, I feel at home here – I am welcomed – I feel it deep in my bones.

The garden has an honest and pure ambience to it, with a discernible quality full of brilliance and spirit! I am extremely grateful I have boarded upon this journey - I feel I cannot commend it highly enough, as I sit here surrounded by so much beauty while treasuring all of its imagery.

XXXIV

While standing gracefully in the skyline, I gaze at
the way the silhouette of trees glint goldenly in
the low sun. I am full of admiration for how they
display such beauty in every season - the soft
new green of spring, the rich deep flutter of
summer, and the golden rust of autumn. While
in winter, they etch the sky with their stoic,
skeletal grandeur.

XXXV

What an abundance of pleasure these natural surroundings bestow upon those who are receptive and open to appreciate! And what an assortment of delights too! Who can compute the countless identifiable trait's one is exposed to? I have attempted to portray the gratification experienced by one whose fervour glows brightly. Golden amber shines onto the garden lawn, in visible shafts of light as a sense of summer dances in the serene sky. And what scents the blossoming buds emanate! How wonderful are the rewards, with the shades and hues that sunrise enlightens upon the flower beds! In its entirety, the garden is resplendent with its potent joy.

Doesn't the demonstration of passion and the optimism of bliss stir the imagination with its lucid perception?

The exhibition of the garden, with our capacity to consider it in its entirety and in each aspect, unlocks a vast arena of joy and purpose in which to discover. Almost immediately, one's inspiration soars over this swarm of indulgence, expanding in capacity and concentration; the unique vibrations connect and merge together sequentially to create fresh and new ones; visions of splendour entwine with the tremors of joy; goodwill strides alongside smiles of happiness. At last, all the insights, all the awareness, and all the experiences become boundless foundations of pleasure, creating vibrant and enjoyable imprints on me!

XXXVI

It is early, and the garden is suitably adorned in
dreamy hues of romantic tones. Opulent colours
cascade in borders bejewelled with delicate
flowers, while a cloud threatens and swells deep
grey as it blows past the horizon's edges. In the
distance, flashes of gold simmer the sky. Then,
over the rooftops, the arc of a rainbow appears,
as I hear a falling bell-like song. And in sight, a
quick flock of golden birds as if fired from some
great bow! They all flock together, a glorious
conjunction of all weathers, as the sunlight that
then breaks over feels sudden and warm!

And showering down - the birds' sprightly call -
as I look up into the sun and birds all at once.
Their bell-like ringing song whistles all around
me as over the treetops they swirl and swerve,
before flying off as quickly as they had come.
And as their contrasting plumage fades, the
garden is peopled with their softly muted song.

XXXVII

It is morning and I am sitting in the glare of the
sunshine as it smiles upon my face. I feel
enthusiastically compliant to its inspiration, while
also indulging in its expression...

I close my eyes
Sweet dreams arise
I listen to the birds
Listening to every musical verse
And in the music and dance
That bursts with complexity and delight
I open my eyes
I see vivid colours, in leaves and in flowers
Amid patterns rejoicing in the garden
And, like an enchanting carpet beneath my feet
The ground becomes alive
Connecting me with the earth, and with the trees
My body becomes one
With the sky and the surroundings
It's motion, it's energy
Falls behind in memory -
And looking up
I see the stars
Red, blue and green
Iridescent colours passing across
Like living jewellery

Luminous inwardly
Breathing and flowing with the same life that's in
me
As all is aligned
Evoking a sense of beauty
Like the teeth of a beautiful woman
As she smiles
Transposing exuberance
As everything comes alive
Within this moment!

TAT TVAM ASI

FROM RICHARD

If you enjoyed this book, please review and share it.

That helps it find its way to those who need it. This would mean a lot to me. Thank you.

And please feel free to email me at:

richardcbower10@gmail.com

Printed in Great Britain
by Amazon

22746613R00066